And think, this heart, all evil shed away,
A pulse in the eternal mind, no less
Gives somewhere back the thoughts
by England given,
Her sights and sounds, dreams happy
as her day;
And laughter learnt of friends;
and gentleness,
In hearts at peace, under an
English heaven.

"The Soldier" by Rupert Brooke,
1887-1915

To Mike - with all my love

Hearts

THE ART OF MAKING GIFTS OF LOVE AND AFFECTION

Juliet Bawden

Photography by Debbie Patterson

SIMON & SCHUSTER

New York London Toronto Sydney Tokyo Singapore

SIMON & SCHUSTER
Simon & Schuster Building
Rockefeller Center
1230 Avenue of the Americas
New York, NY 10020

First published in 1992 by
Conran Octopus Limited
37 Shelton Street,
London WC2H 9HN

Project Editors Denise Bates and
Louise Simpson
Art Editor Mary Evans
Designers Kit Johnson and
Olivia Brooks
Copy Editor Patsy North
Editorial Assistant Jo Mead
Production Alison McIver
Americanisation Maggi McCormick
Calligraphy Jane Thompson
Illustrations Paul Bryant
Needlework charts Eli King
and Candace Bahouth

Typeset by The R & B Partnership
Printed in Hong Kong

10 9 8 7 6 5 4 3 2 1

Library of Congress Cataloging-in-Publication Data

Bawden, Juliet.
    Hearts : The art of making gifts of love and affection /
Juliet Bawden.
       p. cm.
    Includes bibliographical references and index.
    ISBN 0-671-78960-6
    1. Handicraft. 2. Heart in art. I. Title.
TT157.B355 1992
745.594--dc20
                                              92-17873
                                              CIP

CONTENTS

INTRODUCTION

The image of the heart is a potent one. Over the centuries it has evolved from a symbol of power to one of love and friendship. When Cro-magnon man painted the heart on the walls of his cave, it symbolized his desire to gain ultimate control over his enemy. And, of course, prehistoric man realized very quickly that an injury to the heart was always fatal, and equated this organ with both life and death.

The ancient Greeks and Egyptians believed that in the vertical scheme of things there were three focal points in the human body: the brain, the heart, and the sexual organs. Because the heart lies between the other two it was regarded as a sort of crossing point of passion and intellect. In fact, the heart was believed by some to be the seat of intelligence, and the brain merely an instrument of the heart. This led to the analogy of the moon corresponding to the brain and the heart to the sun.

The heart and the sun are both symbols of the essence of life, and the rayed sun and radiant or flaming heart are often used to represent the centres of the macrocosm and the microcosm respectively. Whereas the sun is used to symbolize the centre of heaven, the heart is the centre of man and his very inner essence. In Ancient Egypt, the heart was the only part of the viscera left in the embalmed mummy as it was regarded as indispensible to the body in the After Life.

Religious iconography also makes use of the heart symbol. In Christian art, the flaming heart symbolizes charity and religious zeal, and is often associated with St Augustin and Christ. A heart in the hand portrays love and piety, and a heart pierced by an arrow is indicative of a contrite spirit. A Renaissance emblem also depicts a heart pierced by an arrow with the motto, *Amor vincit omnia*, Love conquers all. Specific religious orders have also adopted the heart as their symbol. The Jesuits use a heart crowned with thorns as their emblem, and the Order of the Bleeding Heart was a semi-religious Medieval sect in honour of the Virgin Mary, whose "heart was pierced with many arrows". The heart also occurs in the Eastern religions. For the Chinese Buddhists, the heart is one of the eight precious organs of the Buddha. It is also embodied in the Tree of Life where it conveys the concept of fertility.

Yet it is principally with romance that people associate the heart as a symbol, and St Valentine's Day is a time when lovers exchange heart gifts or cards. Mid-February has been associated with young love since Roman times, when the festival of Lupercalia celebrated Juno and marriage. Later the Christian church linked this event with the saint day of Valentine, a bishop who was executed in 270 AD for holding weddings against the express edict of the Emperor.

As a shape, the heart is normally a symmetrical image, and obviously a very stylized version of the actual physical heart. This may stem from Central Asia, where the heart symbol reflected inwardly curving animal horns. Hearts are prolific as a decorative symbol in folk art, particularly in Northern Europe. In Scandinavia hearts decorate painted furniture, and in other countries hearts are used on quilts, appliqué, samplers and patchwork. Baby quilts are often decorated with hearts to suggest the strong bond of love between a mother and her child.

The projects in this book cover many of the different meanings of hearts, from the simply decorative to the deeply romantic. Some of the items are inspirational but most are practical projects for you to make up. The fact that all of the items are hand made and that time and care have been taken with them shows that they are all true symbols of love and affection. Hopefully, each item will bring you great pleasure and satisfaction, whether to make for yourself or to give to a loved one.

Home
IS WHERE THE
Heart
IS

In the folk art of many countries, the heart motif has long been used to decorate the home; the Pennsylvania Dutch designs of early American settlers are particularly well known for their deceptively simple yet utterly enticing patterns. The Shakers, with their motto "Hands to work, hearts to God," incorporate the motif in many of their craft pieces. The heart symbol adds an immediate note of warmth wherever it is used, transforming functional items into objects of beauty.

PAPIER-MÂCHÉ MIRROR

Mention papier-mâché to many people, and they will reminisce about early school days, making puppet heads or small brightly colored bowls from bits of newspaper and lots of glue. However, papier-mâché has a long tradition; it has been, and still is, produced all over the world to make many different artifacts. It is manufactured in Kashmir, where it is turned into coasters, trays, and small household items. In the Philippines, animals are made from it, while in Mexico, brightly colored fruits, birds, and figures are made for export.

During the eighteenth and nineteenth centuries in Britain, an industry employing hundreds of people was set up in the Midlands. The popularity of papier-mâché grew with the popularity of imported lacquer or japanned wares. Papier-mâché was made from pressed paper pulp, chalk, and sand mixed with glue and pressed into molds, then baked and painted. The style, colors, and motifs with which these items were painted were those of Japanese lacquer ware. Later the styles changed, and sometimes the papier-mâché was inlaid with mother-of-pearl.

As the interest in papier-mâché grew, people took out patents as they discovered different ways of making it and new uses to which it could be put. These included architectural moldings, which, up to the middle of the eighteenth century, had to be carved in wood by hand, which was both expensive and time-consuming. Charles Bielefeld, an inventor and manufacturer, made papier-mâché panels measuring 6 ft. x 8 ft./1.8 m x 2.4 m, which he used to construct bulkheads and cabin partitions for railroad cars shown in the Great Exhibition of 1851 in London. These were both tough and soundproof. He also made some prefabricated houses out of papier-mâché for a client who was emigrating to Australia. Papier-mâché was made for nose cones of British planes during World War II, since radar could not travel through it. In more recent years, the East German car, the Trabant, was partly made from papier-mâché.

During the last ten years, there has been a new interest in papier-mâché as a craft material. It has many appealing properties: it is inexpensive, you need no specialist equipment, and it is environmentally sound.

Right The finished papier-mâché mirror and matching vase adorned with colorful bathing beauties

MAKING THE MIRROR

Papier-mâché is made in two basic ways. The first method is known as pulping. Here the paper is pulped and then mixed with glue. The second method is layering and is used for this mirror. It is a good idea either to use different colored newspapers for each layer or to write a number on each layer as you complete it.

MATERIALS
LARGE SHEET OF CORRUGATED
CARDBOARD
OLD NEWSPAPERS
ROUND MIRROR
2 "D" RINGS OR SIMILAR FOR HANGING
MODELLING CLAY
WALLPAPER PASTE
STRONG CONTACT ADHESIVE
PAPER GLUE
WHITE LATEX PAINT
ACRYLIC PAINTS
BLACK INK
ACRYLIC VARNISH
SCISSORS
EXACTO KNIFE
PAINTBRUSHES

MAKE A TEMPLATE by placing the mirror on a sheet of paper and drawing around it. Draw a heart shape around the circle, altering it as necessary until you are happy with the proportions. Fold the paper in half down the center of the circle and heart and then cut out, following one side of the heart so that the tem-

Preparing the cardboard heart shapes and clay figures

Inserting a small round mirror and adding "D" rings to the back

Painting the two cardboard hearts and the figures with white latex. Once the latex is completely dry, use acrylic paints for bright colors and sharp detail; finish with a coat of clear varnish

plate is symmetrical. Use the template to cut two shapes from corrugated cardboard. Place the mirror on one of the pieces of cardboard, draw around it and then cut out the circle using an exacto knife. Draw a smaller heart for the cherubs to hold, and cut out from the cardboard.

FROM CLAY, SHAPE three figures. Place them on the large heart template and arrange them until they are the shape you want and lying in a satisfactory position.

USING CONTACT GLUE, attach the "D" rings to the back of the large heart shape without the hole. On the back of the heart shape with the hole, use wallpaper paste to glue narrow strips of newspaper, slightly overlapping, around the edge of the circle, with half the strip extending into the hole. When dry, fold the strips forward onto the front of the heart and then insert the mirror in position from the back.

BRING THE STRIPS back onto the mirror, and place a thin roll of clay just inside the edge of the circle. Moisten the strips with wallpaper paste to soften them and then fold them neatly over the clay to form a lip over the edge of the mirror. Allow to dry. Remove the mirror and use narrow strips of paper to put a second layer over the lip. Allow to dry. Meanwhile, on the clay figures and the small heart, place three layers of papier-mâché by dipping strips of newspaper in wallpaper paste and pasting them, slightly overlapping, all over the shapes.

WHEN DRY, COAT the mirror lip with white latex, then paint it the color of your choice and varnish it. When the varnish is dry, place the mirror in position from the back, so that it is flush with the cardboard. Spread contact glue over the back of the mirror and the heart shape and on the underside of the heart shape with the "D" rings. When the glue is tacky, stick the two pieces together. Add two layers of papier-mâché over the completed heart shape.

WHEN THE FIGURES have completely dried out, cut them in half with an exacto knife and separate the clay from the papier-mâché shell. Glue the two sides of each figure together using contact glue. Work papier-mâché over the seams. When the figures are dry, paint them with white latex. Also paint the large and small hearts with white latex.

WHEN THE LATEX is dry, paint on your design in acrylic paints. Use black ink for detailing features and patterns. Write names, messages, or your own signature in black ink. Place the figures on the frame and mark their positions. Glue the figures in place using contact adhesive. Glue the small heart into the figures' hands. When everything is dry, cover the figures and mirror surround with a coat of clear varnish.

Right The completed mirror

CUPID CUSHION

Needlepoint is a form of embroidery which is worked on canvas. The word canvas comes from the Greek *kannabis*, meaning hemp, and the oldest known surviving example of needlepoint is thought to be a fragment of a stole, dated as pre-thirteenth century. This was unearthed in the nineteenth century from the tomb of Archbishop Hubert Walter at Canterbury Cathedral.

Needlepoint was worked mainly for ecclesiastical purposes until the time of Elizabeth I, when English ladies of leisure took it up as a pastime. They sewed on firm, even-woven canvas with silks and wools using tent stitch. Needlepoint became so popular that the grand households employed professional embroiderers to produce and adapt designs for the lady of the house to work. For centuries, young girls were instructed in needlepoint by their grandmothers and mothers, or by nuns. In Prussia, in 1872, embroidery, along with knitting, mending, and darning, became part of the school curriculum.

At the beginning of the sixteenth century, commercially printed designs became available in books known as sample books. These printed designs could be used for many different forms of needlework, for example, weaving, lacemaking, and filet

work. The drawings were usually supplied with a grid or a graph, just like the ones we use today.

This wonderful pillow, with its romantic and playful cherubs, has been made up in warm and evocative shades of terra cotta and burgundy. The Latin inscription, *Amor Amicitia*, means Love and Friendship.

Above Detail of the right-hand cupid

Right The finished pillow with its warm, blending colors and Latin inscription

MAKING THE CUPID CUSHION

The pillow measures approximately 16 in./40½ cm across by 16½ in./42 cm down, and is made in tapestry yarn, in 19 rich colors. The needlepoint can be worked with half cross stitch or continental tent stitch. Interlock canvas is used for the pillow as it is very strong, with double threads twisted together. The mesh or gauge of the canvas indicates the number of holes in the canvas per inch, and for the pillow a 10-gauge canvas is best.

The ideal yarn to use is specially spun needlepoint wool, as it is less stretchy than knitting yarn. This is divided into two types – tapestry and crewel yarn. Tapestry is a smooth 4-ply yarn, and crewel is a 2-ply yarn. Tapestry yarn is recommended for the pillow, and it is best to use a tapestry needle, which is blunt-ended and slips through the canvas easily without snagging.

It is also a good idea to use a frame when doing needlepoint as this will prevent the canvas from distorting and will make the piece easier to work. You can either buy a tapestry frame at a craft shop, or buy a canvas stretcher from an art shop (it looks rather like a picture frame).

MATERIALS
18 IN² /45 CM² PIECE ÉCRU (BEIGE) CANVAS
(10 GAUGE)
APPLETON'S TAPESTRY YARN
IN 19 SHADES:
SHADES: 976, 965, 152, 987, 125, 204,
121, 227, 757, 929, 747, 746, 821, 455,
102, 355, 401, 695, 696
BLUNT TAPESTRY NEEDLE (SIZE 18)
EMBROIDERY SCISSORS
TAPESTRY FRAME
MASKING TAPE

CUT THE CANVAS 2 in./5 cm larger all around than the size you require. Cover the raw edges with masking tape to prevent any unraveling. Pin the canvas to the canvas frame.

THREAD THE NEEDLE with a double strand of yarn and knot the end. Following the chart, work the design in half cross stitch or continental tent stitch. Each square on the chart represents one stitch. Start the first row at the upper right-hand corner and work each row of stitches from right to left. At the end of the row, turn the canvas upside down and work the stitches of the next row in line with the one below. Each stitch must be taken in the same direction.

NOTE: the needle passes under two vertical threads of canvas.

TO MAKE THE canvas into a pillow, follow the normal method of making a pillow, using a suitably sturdy material as the back. See page 96, A Keepsake Pincushion, for tips on making a tight-fitting and firm pillow cover.

965		746	
152		821	
125		455	
204		102	
121		355	
227		401	
757		696	
929		695	
747		976	
987			

Note: 821 is only used for the forget-me-nots. 125 is only used for the cupid outlines.

HEART RUGS

Rugs have risen in popularity in the last 20 years. They are the perfect complement to fashionable stripped, stained or painted wooden floors. For artists who work in a variety of mediums, including felt, wood, and metal, rugs offer a large area on which to produce an image. These rugs are particularly exciting as the decorative theme has been translated into the actual shape of the rug. The designs are not bound by traditional heart shapes, but instead revel in asymmetric forms. Their ebullient colors and textural variations evoke life and vitality, suggesting the creative force and brilliance of nature itself. When the rug artist has finished the tufting, the rugs are squeezed and curled until they have an organic feel to them. Only then are they ready to be used underfoot.

The technique for making these rugs is a relatively new one, which because of its speed compared with hand-tufting or weaving, has revolutionized rug design and manufacture by artist craftsmen in the last few years. A tufting gun is used to make a pattern or picture using yarn in the same way that a paint brush carries paint. The gun is loaded with yarn, and the yarn design is punched into the canvas. The tufting gun is very versatile and can produce figurative work as well as abstract or geometric designs with areas of flat color and texture. A tool that was originally used for mending rather than making rugs has changed the face and nature of rug design.

To make a gun-tufted rug, a vertical frame is set up with a canvas stretched across it. So that rugs of varying sizes can be made, it is a good idea to have an adjustable frame. The design is drawn on the back of the canvas, as the artist works from this side. The gun is held on a special frame, which in turn is held from a roller bar, attached along the top of the framework so that the gun can be moved freely from side to side and up and down. To make each tuft, the gun is simply pushed forwards to puncture the stretched canvas.

Right A variety of jewel-colored rugs picking out the pastel colors of a gypsy caravan. The larger rug makes a wonderful centerpiece for a living room
Left Gun-tufting creates a richly textured rug and allows intricate patterns

DOLL'S QUILT

This pretty appliqué quilt is made in fine wool in soft colors. Although the pattern is for a doll's quilt, the principles of quilt making are the same for any size of quilt, and this design would be ideal for a baby or young child. Why not make matching child's and doll's quilts? For inspiration, go and have a look at the miniature versions of adult quilts in museum collections (there are many fascinating collections all over America); such quilts were often made by children as sampler quilts, while others were made for dolls.

A quilt normally consists of three layers: a top layer, a filling which is usually batting, and a backing. With patchwork and appliquéd quilts, the top is normally constructed first and then the three layers are assembled to produce the finished quilt.

Once you have decided on the basic design, you can then work out the size of the quilt. The size of the basic blocks and the elements contained within them will depend on whether the quilt is for a crib or a cradle, or for an adult bed. Here is a rough guide to quilt sizes:
Cradle: 27 in. x 50 in./68 cm x 127 cm
Crib: 30 in. x 75 in./76 cm x 190 cm
It is best to be fairly flexible about the size of the quilt as, to a certain extent, the size of the pattern will determine its dimensions and not the other way around. You will find that this is especially true when making patchwork quilts.

CALCULATING FABRIC REQUIREMENTS

If you are using fabric scraps, you will not have to work out exact fabric requirements. However, if you are starting from scratch, you will need to know how much fabric to buy in any one pattern or color. You will need as much batting and backing fabric as the size of your finished quilt plus its border.

The choice of fabric is all important. Although we have used new fabrics for the doll's quilt, old and faded fabrics work particularly well. Collect fabric from wherever you can – yard sales, secondhand stores, old garments, etc. Then match complementary colors and patterns, achieving a mixture of dark, light, medium shades and throughout the design if you are using different prints.

You do not need to be an expert seamstress, as a simple overcast stitch is all that is required here.

Left This beautiful doll's quilt is made from fresh gingham checks and floral cotton hearts

MATERIALS
TEMPLATES (SEE PAGE 125)
PENCIL AND PAPER
FINE WOOL OR COTTON IN VARIOUS
COLORS AND PATTERNS
BATTING
BACKING FABRIC
THREAD
NEEDLE AND PINS
DRESSMAKING SHEARS

CUT OUT A heart shape from paper (see page 125 for a suitable template). Using the paper heart as a template, pin it on a piece of fabric to be used for the appliqué and draw around it. Then add a border of 1/4 in./6 mm all the way around for turning under. Repeat for all the other hearts.

CUT OUT AS many fabric rectangles as you need. Each should be large enough for a heart to fit into with a surrounding border.

IRON EACH FABRIC piece flat and turn the 1/4 in./5 mm border under so that it will be easier to sew. Pin each heart shape to its background fabric and sew into position with overcast stitches (or running stitch if you prefer). Arrange the hearts together to form a pleasing composition and then sew the first row of rectangles together across the width of the quilt, turn-

Above Small floral prints and gingham checks in cotton or a cotton mix are perfect for a doll's quilt where the small scale is essential
Right Detail of the finished quilt

ing the edges under. Sew the next and subsequent rows in the same way. When these strips are complete, sew them together to form the quilt.

CUT A STRIP of fabric about 4 3/4 in./12 cm wide to form the border. This can be sewn on by hand or by machine.

FINALLY CUT OUT a piece of backing fabric and a piece of batting the same size as the quilt top plus the border. Lay the quilt top right-side up on the batting and baste the two layers together as close to the edge as possible. With right sides facing, place the backing fabric on the lining fabric and sew around the edge, leaving a gap through which to turn the quilt right side out. Turn the quilt and blindstitch to close the gap.

SWEETHEART QUILT

This luxurious patchwork quilt is made from a combination of cream silk and maroon velvet patchwork. A row of maroon velvet hearts surrounded by gold beads of decreasing size border the patchwork squares.

Making a two-tone quilt based on a square design is not only very simple, but also extremely striking. You don't have to use silk and velvets as we have done here, but try crisp, contrasting cottons or striped mattress ticking. If you are making a quilt for a twin bed (approximately 39 x 75 in./100 x 190 cm), you will need about 3¼ yd./3 m of the darker color and about 5½ yd./5 m of the lighter color (you need more of this for the border). For a double bed (approximately 54 x 75 in./137 x 190 cm) you will need 4⅜ yd./4 m of the darker color and 7½ yd./7 m of the lighter.

MAKING THE QUILT

The quilt is made by hand in traditional English patchwork fashion, with paper templates forming the basis of the squares. The quantities given are based on a twin bed.

The sumptuous sweetheart quilt made in velvet and silk

MATERIALS
5½ YD./5 M LIGHT FABRIC
3¼ YD./3 M DARK FABRIC
QUILT BATTING THE SAME
SIZE AS FINISHED QUILT
SOLID COTTON OR SINGLE FLAT SHEET
FOR BACKING
CARDBOARD OR METAL TEMPLATE
MAGAZINE PAPER FOR TEMPLATES
DRESSMAKING SHEARS
DRESSMAKER'S PINS
NEEDLE AND THREAD
SET SQUARE
IRON

FIRST DECIDE HOW large you want to make each square and make a rigid template from lightweight cardboard. Make sure your template is absolutely 90° square by checking each corner with a set square. If you are at all unsure about your geometry, it is better to buy a metal template, which will last you for years.

NEXT DRAW AROUND your template on magazine paper – this needs to be firm enough to hold the shape of the fabric, but thin enough to sew through. Slick magazine paper is ideal.

PLACE THE PAPER templates on the fabric with the appropriate seam allowances between each piece. Place a pin in the center of each piece and cut out the shape including seam allowances (about ½ in./1 cm). Fold the seam allowance of the fabric in and baste it the paper template. Iron each piece flat.

ONCE YOU HAVE several squares of different colors ready, you can start to sew them together. It is better to work one block at a time; you can carry small pieces around with you, working on them in spare moments.

TO SEW THE pieces together, hold two patches with right sides facing and oversew the edges using very tiny, neat stitches. At the corners add a few extra stitches of reinforcement. Once the pattern is complete, remove the basting and pull out the paper templates gently.

MAKE A BORDER from four strips of the pale fabric and sew it around the edge of the patches. Then baste a piece of quilt batting to the back, securing it around the edges and also in the middle.

FOR THE BACKING fabric, use a twin-bed flat cotton sheet or even lining fabric. You need enough to cover the quilt completely with an inch or two for a seam allowance. Place the backing fabric with its right side against the right side of the patchwork, and baste and then sew around three and a half sides. Leave a gap in one of the short sides to turn the quilt right side out.

NEXT TRIM THE corners and remove basting and pins and turn right side out. Close the gap with blindstitch or slip stitching. To stop the batting

Cutting out your heart shape from firm magazine paper or thin cardboard

Covering the paper heart with velvet and fusible interfacing

Basting through the fabric and paper with thread

Right Detail of beaded velvet hearts appliquéd on to the quilt

from slipping, sew a tiny gold bead through the three layers of quilt at each corner of each square.

WITH THE LEFTOVER darker fabric (in this case velvet), you can now make the stunning appliqué hearts. As velvet is tricky to sew, it is a good idea to use a fusible interfacing to help stiffen the fabric to prevent it from moving around too much.

FIRST MAKE A heart template from cardboard – it looks best if the heart is quite rounded and has a deep V (see page 126 for a suitable template). Trace this on magazine paper, making enough paper templates to border the quilt. You will want to make about 25 hearts altogether.

IRON THE FUSIBLE interfacing onto the back of the velvet and peel off the backing paper. Cut out a velvet heart which is approximately ½ in./1 cm wider than the paper heart. Pin the paper in the center of the interlining and then baste the fabric on the paper. Fold the edges in to give a heart shape. Snip into the V of the heart so that you can get a close fit around the paper and then dab it with a spot of glue to stop fraying.

BASTE THE VELVET heart, pushing the needle through the paper template. Sew it on the border of the quilt, but not through the paper template. Leave a small space through which to remove the paper once the basting has been snipped and pulled away. Close the gap by overcasting. Surround each heart with gold beads.

BATHROOM HEARTS

A bathroom can be one of the most pleasurable rooms in a house, giving a chance to show off your eye for detail. Decorate hand towels with cross-stitch hearts. Collect small heart-shaped soaps and display them in a pretty dish or stencil a border of hearts around the bathtub. Cut a heart shape from sponge and use it to apply paint to ceramic tiles. You could also make a heart stencil to go around the walls or across your tiles in your chosen color scheme.

Top left Cross-stitched heart on a plain white cloth; *Top right* Heart-shaped glycerine soaps

Baby Love

The arrival of a baby has traditionally been, and still is, a time of great joy and, with it, industry. We want to welcome the new baby into the world with something special made out of love – a gift that cannot be mass-produced. There are many customs and superstitions surrounding birth. Gifts of clothing are common, as is the giving of silver, which is believed to be a way of warding off evil. Sometimes the silver is a piece of jewelry, or it might be a spoon, napkin ring, or a teething ring, from which a silver heart may hang.

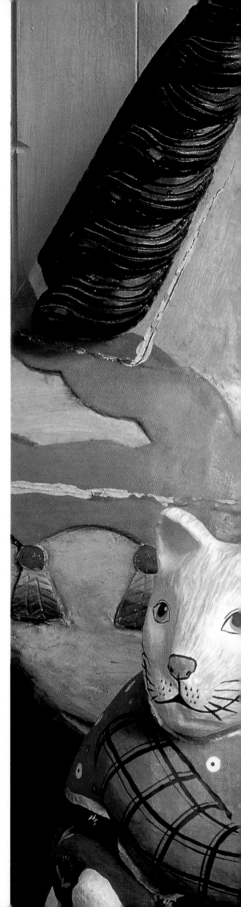

STENCILED TOY BOX

Stenciling is believed to have originated in Egypt as early as 2500 B.C. It is thought to have been in France, during the Middle Ages, that the word "stenciling" evolved from the word *estenceler*, which means "to sparkle." This was because the French added sparkling decorations through stencils to their wallpapers, books, fabrics, and playing cards.

During the late sixteenth and early seventeenth centuries, stenciling was used regularly to decorate the homes of the rich. At about the same time that the early settlers were arriving in North America. Missing the decorations of their former homes, they took to stenciling their floors, walls, and furnishings. It was in America that the itinerant stenciler would travel from town to town carrying stencils cut from leather or heavy cardboard covered with candlewax, and pigments in leather pouches. The recurrent motifs of folk art (flowers, hearts, birds, animals, and scenes

*Above Details of the sides of the toy chest,
with stenciled hearts and arrows
Right The completed chest is ideal for storing
children's clothes or toys*

from the Bible) are found in stenciling as far apart as Scandinavia, the European Alps, and the American east coast.

Since these early stencils, life has become much easier. There are now special brushes, paints, pens, and clear plastic acetate which all make the task of a stenciler more straightforward. We are surrounded by patterns, too. Look at wallpaper, china, fabrics, flowers and seashells, and the intricate designs on fish and animal skins. Our toy box uses a fairly simple motif, which was inspired by the appliquéd overalls on page 36.

MAKING THE STENCILED TOY BOX

Although we have given our toy box a base color, you can, of course, paint or stencil the design directly on the wood. It is important to make sure that all decorative finishes are painted on clean, bare wood which has first been sanded and filled where necessary, scrubbed, and rubbed with turpentine. Unless you have a steady hand or are an expert at painting, it is a good idea to remove any handles before beginning to paint.

You may wish to lighten or bleach the color of the wood. To lighten the color, apply a coat of white oil-based paint. Wait for a few minutes and then rub it off with a rag. You will be left with white residue in

the cracks and knots which makes a good base for your design. Alternatively, you can scrub the box with household bleach and then rinse it well with water.

Above and right Details of the stenciled decorations. For the stencil template, see page 126

Another treatment for wood is to dye or stain it. You can use ordinary fabric or carpet dyes; the intensity of the finished color depends on how dilute you make it, and how many coats you paint on. Stains go deeper into the wood than dyes and should be used with caution. They come in a choice of natural wood colors from pale ash blond to dark oak. You can also get stains in colors such as blue, green, or red. Before dyeing or staining the box, do a test piece on the base of the box to check the intensity of the color and to make sure that the stain and paints you are using are compatible. Use specialist acrylic paints for wood as they are quick-drying, or ordinary satin wood paint, latex or gloss, although the latter can have a very hard look to it.

MATERIALS
AN UNPAINTED, UNVARNISHED
TOY CHEST
SANDPAPER
PRIMER
UNDERCOAT
DARK BLUE LATEX
STENCILS (SEE PAGE 126 FOR HEARTS
AND ARROWS DESIGN AND PAGE 124 FOR
MAKING THE STENCILS)
PAINTS
PAINT BRUSHES
SAUCER OR PALETTE
GOLD PAINT
GOLD FELT-TIPPED PEN
SPRAY ADHESIVE
MATTE POLYURETHANE VARNISH

SAND DOWN ANY rough edges on the chest and then wipe away any dust, so you have a clean, dust-free surface on which to work. Give the chest a coat of primer, leave to dry, and then sand down. Then paint with undercoat, leave to dry, and sand down again. Now give the chest a coat of latex and allow to dry. If the color is not dark enough, give it another coat of latex.

STENCIL THE HEARTS and arrows randomly over the box. Use bright colors for the hearts and orange for the arrows. Add any freehand details such as dots and stripes using a finer brush. Mix the colors as you need them on a saucer or palette. Stencil over the arrows in gold, letting some of the orange color show through. Draw a border line along the lid and the sides of the box with a gold felt-tipped pen.

SPRAY THE FINE details with a spray adhesive before painting the rest of the toy box with a matte polyurethane varnish to protect it.

T O D D L E R S ' T O G S

APPLIQUÉD CLOTHES

Appliqué is the name given to sewing pieces of fabric onto a fabric background for either decorative or functional purposes. Appliqué has served many different purposes throughout history, from saddle covers used by nomadic cattle breeding tribes who wandered the Gobi Desert as far back as 200 B.C., to decorated banners carried by troops of all nations going into battle.

Between 300 and 1000 A.D., the Copts of Egypt used overlay appliqué to decorate robes. During the Middle Ages in Europe, inlaid appliqué was used as a substitute for embroidery for household furnishings, banners, and military and ecclesiastical clothing. In India, too, appliqué has been practiced for centuries. The craft of leather appliqué was used particularly for covering shields in Kutch and Sind (now Pakistan).

You can use appliqué to decorate all manner of things from garments to pictures. You can make appliqué pockets or a motif to go on the back of a denim jacket. Appliqué a patch over a hole in a garment or use it to strengthen knees and elbows. Because it can be colorful and very hard-wearing, appliqué is particularly suitable for decorating toddlers' clothes.

WORKING THE APPLIQUÉ

These denim overalls have been decorated with attractive primary-colored hearts to pick up their rainbow-striped straps. In fact, this much-loved and much-worn garment inspired the decoration of the toy box on page 33.

Left and above Bought dungarees can be cheaply and easily enlivened with brightly colored fabric hearts

MATERIALS
PAPER
PENCIL
SCISSORS
FABRIC SCRAPS
DRESSMAKING SHEARS
SEWING THREAD TO MATCH
NEEDLE AND PINS

FIRST, DRAW YOUR design on paper or cut out hearts from colored paper, arranging and rearranging them until you have a pleasing composition. Draw around the hearts on the background fabric to remind you where to place each fabric shape. Using a paper heart as a template, cut out fabric hearts; add 1/4 in./5 mm all around for turning under the edges if you are working the appliqué by hand.

MAKE LITTLE SNIPS all around the edge of your shape with a pair of scissors. This will help to ease the fabric when turning it under – particularly important with the curves in a heart shape. Turn the edge under by 1/4 in./5 mm and baste. Sew each piece in position. When you are sewing one heart on top of another, always pin and sew the larger one in position first of all.

IF YOU ARE stitching the appliqué by machine, you will not need any extra fabric around the edge for turning under. Pin the heart shape into position on the background fabric, then work running stitch by hand as close to the edge as possible. Set your machine to a close zigzag (satin) stitch and sew around the shape, covering the raw edge and the line of running stitch as you go.

BEADED DENIMS

Beads are one of the oldest forms of decorative art. Evidence of their use has been found dating back over 7,000 years to the early civilizations of Mesopotamia (Iraq) and Egypt. It was the Egyptians who first developed the art of bead embroidery to decorate their mummies. Beads are often worn to show status and wealth, and in many cultures, beads are worn for pro-

tection against evil spirits or as good luck charms.

The Victorians and Edwardians used beads to decorate accessories such as parasols, gloves, bags, caps, and shoes. These tiny sneakers in vivid pink decorated with tiny pearls and a red heart on each ankle are a far cry from formal Victorian shoes. The simple shift dresses of the 1920s were often decorated with sequins arranged in patterns or depicting stylized flowers and birds. After the austerity years of World War II, there was a renewal of interest in bead work, which resulted in the flamboyant creations on couturier gowns in the early 1950s. Later that decade, lambswool sweaters and cardigans with elaborate patterns of bead work became very fashionable.

When working with beads, you will need to use strong sewing thread and a beading needle, which is particularly long and fine. Beads may be bought in bulk already threaded on strings, which makes them easier to thread on the needle. Or pin the thread holding the beads on the garment and then catch the thread between each bead and sew them on to the garment. Before starting to sew beads, place them next to one another and try out different combinations for size and color. Beaded hearts can look particularly effective if you create the apex or indentation of the heart with a larger or smaller bead.

Right Beaded denims and pink sneakers decorated with pink hearts and small glass beads

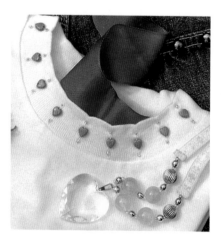

The neckline of this white T-shirt is emphasized with pretty heart beads

A stunning beaded heart individualizes a denim jacket

Pretty loops of beads and crystal hearts embellish a child's skirt

Above Baby bootees decorated with little
sateen appliqué hearts

Right A single chain-stitch heart completes this
delicate christening bonnet

Traditionally, baby clothes were made in pale colors, which lend themselves particularly well to delicate embroidery. This christening set of bootees, baby bonnet, robe, and petticoat is adorned with tiny pin tucks, seed pearls, old lace and fine embroidery. A number of ideas are shown here, which you can then adapt to the clothes that you would like to embroider yourself. It is most effective to use pale colors which complement this very delicate sort of decoration. Highly patterned fabrics would spoil the appliqué.

MATERIALS
EMBROIDERY THREAD
SEED PEARLS
LACE
INTERLINING
SATEEN COTTON
NEEDLE AND PINS

THE CHRISTENING ROBE itself is multi-layered, with lines of creamy lace dividing each layer. The yoke is made from panels of the minutest pin tucks interspersed with detailed embroidery of French knots, trellis stitch and chain-stitch hearts facing one another in repeated rows.

THE CHRISTENING UNDERSKIRT has a heart cut from sateen cotton on the yoke. Cut out the heart shape from the fabric, turn the edges under and sew the heart into place using blanket stitch. A quilted effect is achieved over the heart by the use of back stitches in a grid pattern. Work a French knot on each intersection to give a delicate textural variation.

THE BOOTEES, WHICH are made from quilted satin, continue the theme. From interlining, cut a heart shape large enough to fit on the front of the bootee and cut a slightly larger heart shape from sateen cotton. Cut a piece of lace and sew the two ends together to form a circle. Work a line of running stitches around one edge and gather the lace.

SEW THE GATHERED lace circle on to the front of the bootee. Place the larger heart over the smaller interlining heart and sew the edges under. Cut out a decorative motif from within the pattern of your lace and stitch it into the center of each heart adding a line of three seed pearls. Then sew the heart on to the center of the gathered lace circle.

THE BONNET IS made of ivory-colored fine sateen cotton, with a deep gathered lace trim surrounding the face, and ties with satin ribbon. To add the decoration in one corner, sew a heart shape in chain stitch and then sew seed pearls on to this. A tiny lace bow can finally be added to the center.

CROSS-STITCH SAMPLER

Although there is evidence that samplers were in existence in Asia during the ninth century, it was not until the sixteenth century that they first appeared in Europe. They were originally used as a personal dictionary of stitches and as directories of patterns for future handiwork. Often carried out by high-ranking ladies of society, they were a highly prized art form.

The fabric traditionally used for samplers was linen. It is best to use a fabric with an even weave, so that the threads can be counted easily. Popular modern fabrics are Aida, linen, and hardanger cloth. This sampler was worked in stranded embroidery floss. You can use two or three of the six strands, depending on how dense you wish the color to be.

A round embroidery hoop with a screw-type tension adjuster is ideal for cross stitch. Place the area to be worked over the inner ring and gently push the outer ring over it, so the fabric is held taut.

Right The finished sampler
Far right Each square on the chart represents one square on the fabric

MATERIALS
11-COUNT AIDA FABRIC MEASURING
16½ IN./42 CM SQUARE
1 SKEIN OF STRANDED COTTON IN EACH
OF THE FOLLOWING COLORS:
DARK BLUE FOR OUTLINE; MID BLUE FOR
ALPHABET; LIGHT BLUE FOR MOTIFS
TAPESTRY NEEDLE NO. 24 OR 26
EMBROIDERY SCISSORS
EMBROIDERY HOOP
CARDBOARD FOR MOUNTING

IF YOU WANT to use a finer Aida fabric, you can work out the size of the finished embroidery. Count the number of squares across the chart to work out the width of the tapestry, and the number of squares down to work out the depth. Divide each by the number of threads per 1 in./2.5 cm in the fabric you intend to use.

CUT THE FABRIC at least 2 in./5 cm wider each way than the finished size to allow for turning under when finishing. Machine or overcast the edges to prevent fraying.

FIND THE CENTER of the fabric by folding it in half first vertically and then horizontally. Mark the center with a line of basting stitches both lengthways and widthways. It is preferable to start cross stitch at the top of the design. To find the top, count the squares up from the center of the chart and then the number of holes up from the center of the fabric. Make sure the fabric is held tightly in the embroidery frame.

TO WORK IN cross stitch: bring the thread through at the lower right-hand side, leaving a short length of thread on the underside of the work and anchoring it with the first few stitches. Insert the needle across the mesh into the next hole above and diagonally to the left and bring it out behind the fabric. Half the stitch is now made; continue in the same way until the end of the row. Complete the upper half of the stitch by returning in the opposite direction.

TO MOUNT THE sampler, cut a piece of cardboard the correct size and place the finished embroidery over it. If necessary, press the sampler on the back through a damp cloth. Fold the surplus fabric over the back of the cardboard and pin it with drawing pins. Lace the back from side to side and from top to bottom, then remove the drawing pins. The sampler is now finished and ready to hang in a child's bedroom or nursery.

Hearty Feasts

There is an old saying that "food equals love". It is often put into practice in the poorest countries in the world, where with only the bare minimum to eat a family will show their love and hospitality to both friends and strangers by sharing their food. In Germany large heart-shaped cookies decorated with piped icing messages are hung up at Christmas time. The dough from which these cookies are made is known as Lebkuchen, which means life cakes. Why not make a truly romantic dinner of heart-shaped food, and decorate your table with our hand-painted heart plates and delicately stitched table mats.

THE FOOD OF LOVE

Valentine's Day, a birthday, special anniversary, or a simple dinner *à deux* all offer the perfect opportunity to indulge someone close with lovingly prepared heart-shaped food. To go with the recipes here, it is also possible to buy ready-made heart-shaped food, such as the delicate French cheeses from Neufchâtel.

Heart-shaped cake pans and cookie cutters offer endless possibilities and are invaluable tools for the creation of romantic repasts. From main courses to desserts and festive decorations, a little imagination will add a glow to those special meals.

HEARTS AND FLOWERS SALAD
SERVES 2

1 LARGE POTATO, THINLY SLICED
2 LARGE PLUM TOMATOES,
SKINNED AND SEEDED
2 LARGE SLICES SALAMI
2 SLICES COOKED HAM
3 OZ./75 G THINLY SLICED COLD
CHICKEN OR PORK
2 SLICES (/1½–2OZ./40–50 G)
EDAM CHEESE
2 SMALL COOKED BEETS,
THINLY SLICED
1 YELLOW PEPPER, BLANCHED
AND SKINNED

1 LARGE CARROT, THINLY
SLICED LENGTHWISE
4 OZ./100 G ASSORTED
GREEN SALAD LEAVES
8–12 EDIBLE FLOWERS SUCH
AS BORAGE, VIOLAS, OR PANSIES
VINAIGRETTE DRESSING

Cut out as many small heart shapes (1½ in./4 cm at the longest point) as possible from the potato slices using a cookie cutter and steam for about 7 minutes until tender. Leave to cool.

Cut out as many of the same size heart shapes as possible from the tomatoes, salami, ham, chicken or pork and cheese. Then cut out as many tiny heart shapes (1 in./2.5 cm at the longest point) as possible from the beets, peppers, and carrot.

Wash and thoroughly dry the salad leaves. Tear the leaves into bite-size pieces, and place in a large bowl with all the prepared heart shapes and flowers. Toss lightly with sufficient vinaigrette dressing to just coat the salad, taking care with the delicate shapes, and serve at once.

Right Fish garnished with anchovy butter hearts and chives, served with a hearts and flowers salad and lightly steamed vegetables
Overleaf Nut meringue hearts with coffee sauce, strawberry heart tart, and hanging hearts

FISH WITH ANCHOVY BUTTER
SERVES 2

1 WHITE FISH (1½ LB/700 G), FILETED
MELTED BUTTER
SALT AND PEPPER
4 CHIVE STEMS, TO GARNISH

ANCHOVY BUTTER
2 OZ./50 G UNSALTED BUTTER
4 CANNED ANCHOVIES
1 TSP./5 ML CAPERS
½ TSP./2.5 ML LEMON JUICE

For the anchovy butter, blend all the ingredients in a food processor until smooth. Season with pepper to taste. Spread the butter in the center of a small plate and chill until solid. Cut out 4 small heart shapes (1½ in./4 cm at the longest point) using a cookie cutter, and chill.

Wash and dry the filets, then use scissors to reshape the filets slightly to make heart shapes. Brush with melted butter and season. Place on a lightly buttered baking pan and cook under a preheated broiler on medium-high setting for no more than 5 minutes. The fish will be opaque and firm to the touch when cooked.

Garnish with anchovy butter hearts and chives.

HANGING HEARTS

These simple cookies make perfect Christmas tree decorations.

6 OZ./175 G ALL-PURPOSE FLOUR
4 OZ./100 G BUTTER, SOFTENED
2 OZ./50 G SUPERFINE SUGAR
1 TBS./15 ML MILK
15 HARD CANDIES
15 LENGTHS OF THIN RIBBON

Sift the flour into a bowl and rub in the butter until the mixture resembles fine crumbs. Stir in the sugar and milk and work the mixture to a firm dough. Cover with plastic wrap and chill for 15 minutes.

On a floured work surface, roll out the dough about ¼ in./6 mm thick and cut out 15 heart shapes (2½ in./6.5 cm at the longest point). Place on baking pans lined with foil. Using a cutter, cut out the center of each heart and replace it with a piece of candy. With a skewer, make a small hole at the top of each heart.

Chill the shapes for at least 30 minutes. Preheat the oven to 350°F/180°C then bake the shapes for 20–25 minutes until light golden. Re-shape the holes with a skewer while still warm. Leave the cookies to go cold on the pans to cool completely, then peel off and thread with ribbons.

Right Hanging heart cookies, heart-shaped food, and ice cubes

LOVING PLATES

From the early days of history, man has decorated ceramic vessels, and clay decorated with natural pigments dating back to Neolithic times has been found. Chinese, Persian, and English craftsmen have all had a profound effect on the development of ceramics, and today there is a great variety of patterns to inspire you.

These striking heart plates are very simple to do, as they are bought plates decorated with water-based paints. The advantages of such paints is that you do not need a kiln to dry or seal them. Anyone with an oven should be able to achieve the same effect, and the paints are durable and brilliantly colored, brighter than solvent-based equivalents.

You can dilute water-based paints with up to 20 percent water – any more and they become too thin. Apply the paint to either glazed or unglazed ceramics, but do not use it on items that you will eat or drink from. If you want items to be safe for food, you must glaze your ceramics and bake them in a kiln. Water-based paints will not survive the high temperature of a kiln and are only suitable for items such as vases, tiles, and wall plates that do not come into contact with food.

Left Vibrant hand-painted plates

DRYING AND BAKING

When you have applied your paint, leave the object to dry thoroughly (either overnight or up to four days if the paint is really thick). Then place your object in a cold oven and heat to 400°F/200°C for at least 30 minutes and up to 2 hours. Turn the oven off and leave the item inside to cool.

It is a good idea to test a project before you begin to paint it finally. Try out your paint colors on a chipped plate or tile, leave it to dry, and then bake it. If the object comes out brown, the oven is too high or the object has been in too long. Adjust your method accordingly. If you have not dried your item long enough, or the temperature is too low, you will get cracking or blistering.

It is also very important to dry and bake your item every time you apply a new layer of paint, so that each layer is sealed.

HAND PAINTING A HEART PLATE

These lovely plates have an informal freehand design. Don't worry about exact shapes.

NB Do remember that plates are for decorative purposes only, not for food.

MATERIALS

CLOTH TAPEMEASURE
COMPASS
PENCIL
TRACING PAPER
PAPER SCISSORS OR EXACTO KNIFE
CARBON PAPER
MASKING TAPE
MEDIUM AND FINE PAINTBRUSHES
FELT-TIPPED PEN
PLAIN WHITE CERAMIC PLATE
WATER-BASED CERAMIC PAINTS IN
FOUR COLORS (RED, YELLOW,
GREEN, AND WHITE)
SAUCERS OF WATER

MEASURE THE DIAMETER of the center circle of the plate using a cloth tapemeasure. Take a compass and draw the circle on a piece of tracing paper. Draw a circle the same size on carbon paper and cut it out. You can either draw your heart design straight on the tracing paper, or draw it first and then trace it. If you prefer to copy a heart, use the motifs at the back of the book or find a heart image on a Valentine card.

LAY THE CARBON paper circle carbon side down in position on the plate, holding it in place with small pieces of masking tape. Lay the tracing paper circle with your design on it over the top of this, also holding it in place with masking tape.

NOW, USING A hard pencil, draw over the design, transferring it onto the plate. When finished, take off the tracing paper and the carbon paper.

Transfer the pattern onto a plain white plate using tracing paper. Keep your design as fluid and relaxed as possible

Apply the water-based paint in stages. Leave to dry overnight before baking to seal each layer

Paint the rim of the plate carefully and with a steady hand

Right The finished plate

WITH A PEN, mark a point ¼ in./ 0.5 cm in from the outer edge of the plate. Then work your way around the plate, marking points every 1 in./2.5 cm along. This gives you a guideline to follow for your border. With a medium paintbrush, paint the green border, following the dots and leaving the outer edge white (this is for the red rim). Leave to dry for at least 30 minutes.

NOW PAINT THE green areas of the design in the center of the plate. Leave to dry overnight and then bake in an oven as explained, once you have done your test plate and are satisfied that you have the right temperature and the right drying time.

NEXT PAINT THE red heart details and the areas around the hearts. It does not matter if your painting is not perfect – in fact, it adds to the effect! Paint the rim of the plate in red. Leave it to dry overnight and then bake again as above. Paint all the yellow areas next, using the picture of the finished plate for reference. Leave to dry overnight and then bake again. Take a fine paintbrush and white paint, and paint the dots on the areas of the hearts as shown. Also paint the rim with dots. Leave to dry overnight.

LAST, AGAIN USING a fine paintbrush, paint the outlines around the heart shapes, using the carbon markings as your guidelines. Also paint the black edge around the center where the green and red meet. Leave to dry overnight and bake for the last time.

WEAR YOUR Heart ON YOUR Sleeve

L ong ago hearts were embroidered, appliquéd and woven onto court costumes and armor. Between the seventeenth and eighteenth centuries, they were an important symbol in jewelry making, often inscribed with a tender message: "Noe heart more true then mine to your."

Many modern artists and craftsmen use the heart as a motif because it is such a powerful symbol and one that may take many forms. Embroider it on handkerchiefs, paint it on lingerie, or knit it on a sweater.

ARCTIC DREAMS SWEATER

This lovely warm "Arctic Dreams" sweater uses a heart motif combined with Inuit-style designs. It is very striking and will fit bust 32-38 inches, suiting different age groups.

MATERIALS

16 X 1³/₄ OZ. (82 YD.) BALLS OF CREAM
KNITTING WORSTED, COLOR A
4 X 1³/₄ OZ. (82 YD.) BALLS OF BLACK
KNITTING WORSTED, COLOR B
LARGE NEEDLES: 1 PAIR SIZE 8
SMALL NEEDLES: 1 PAIR SIZE 6

MEASUREMENTS

TO FIT BUST: 32-38 IN./82-97 CM
ACTUAL MEASUREMENTS
BUST: 47 IN./120 CM
LENGTH: 25¹/₂ IN./65 CM
SLEEVE : 17 IN./43 CM

GAUGE

18 sts and 24 rows to 4 in./10 cm stockinette st, on large needles.

Left The designs are completed with simple embroidery; a chain-stitch cross on the fish, and a chain-stitch circle and French knot on the star

PAPIER-MÂCHÉ JEWELS

Surely no craft worker uses the heart more prolifically than the jeweler? Incorporated into rings, necklaces, brooches, and bracelets, the heart can take the form of jet, precious metal, pewter, alloys, ceramics, and gems. Engagement rings often incorporate the heart image, and the Victorians traditionally kept a lock of their sweetheart's hair in a heart-shaped locket.

Probably the earliest piece of jewelry to use the heart as a symbol is the scarab that was found in the tomb of Nubkheperre Inyotef, one of the later seventeenth-dynasty Egyptian kings. The heart scarab, which was always made of a green stone, was placed over the heart of the mummy to protect the spirit in the afterlife and guarantee that it would enjoy everlasting happiness.

Here, however, is some less traditional heart jewelry. Made from papier-mâché, these stunning earrings and brooch are lightweight and simple to make. Your design can be as bright or as abstract as you choose. The method of making is very similar to the papier-mâché mirror (page 10).

Cut your jewelry shapes from cardboard and cover with papier-mâché layers, leaving to dry between each layer

Coat the finished papier-mâché with white paint and draw on your design in pencil before painting both front and back of the piece

The finished earring coated with glue and water

Left A cornucopia of heart-shaped jewelry

MATERIALS
CARDBOARD
PAPER SCISSORS
WHITE GLUE
OLD NEWSPAPERS
WHITE POSTER PAINT OR LATEX
BROOCH BACK OR EARRING FINDINGS
WATERCOLOR OR ACRYLIC PAINTS
FOIL (OPTIONAL)

FIRST CUT THE shape of the brooch or earrings from cardboard. Dilute the glue in the proportion of one-third water to two-thirds glue, until the mixture is runny. Tear the newspaper into strips, coat them with the water/glue mixture, and use them to cover the cardboard shape. Leave each coat of paper and glue to dry before applying the next one. The glue will dry very quickly. To speed up the drying, the pieces can be put in a warm place.

WHEN SIX COATS of papier-mâché have been applied and are completely dry, apply a coat of white poster paint or latex to both the front and back of the pieces. When the paint is dry, draw the design on in pencil.

NEXT, GLUE THE heart shape onto the back of the brooch or earring finding. When the glue is dry, cover the glued edge of the jewelry finding with more white papier-mâché for a neat finish. When the whole piece is dry, the design can be painted on. Finish the brooch or earring with a coat of glue and water, which will give a gloss similar to varnish.

GOLD
THREAD
HEARTS

Machine embroidery is a technique whereby you use the sewing machine to "draw" on your material, and so create a design with brightly colored threads, or trace an existing design printed or appliquéd on the fabric. The tie and the handkerchief are simple projects with appliqué hearts decorated with machine-embroidered gold thread arrows. The jewelry is a more complex project, as you use the sewing machine to cover the outline of the brooch completely, and the intensity of the work does take a little more time.

USING THE SEWING MACHINE

For the tie and hanky you can just thread the machine as normal with gold thread in the bobbin and transparent thread in the top spool. This keeps the thread from breaking. Always work from the back so that the gold is on top.

For the jewelry, drop the feed dog teeth on the sewing machine and turn

Left Gold thread heart brooches

77

PAINTED SILK LINGERIE

Although silk painting is not too expensive as a craft, as you need very little in the way of specialist equipment, silk is not cheap. So it is worth experimenting on a remnant of silk before you start on your expensive lingerie. If you do not wish to buy lingerie, you can quite easily make it yourself. Cut out the pattern pieces and paint them before you sew them together.

MATERIALS

SILK PAINTS In the past silk painting was solely the prerogative of the professional, as the materials were not only expensive and hard to come by, but space-consuming steaming equipment was needed to fix the products.

However, in recent years paints have been developed with the keen amateur in mind. Depending on the manufacture of the paints, they may be fixed by ironing on the back of the finished piece or by being dipped in fixative.

Gutta is a blocking agent used to break up areas of color. Add a few drops of gutta solvent if the gutta is too thick. Make sure you do not add too much, or the gutta will bleed and not act as a barrier to the dyes. For different colored gutta, add a few drops of glass paint.

EQUIPMENT

FRAMES You will need an adjustable wooden frame, as the silk must be held tight in order to paint properly. If you do not have an adjustable wooden frame, use an old picture frame or canvas stretchers.

PINS There are special three-pronged flat-sided pins called silk pins that can be used to stretch the silk on the frame. These are better than thumbtacks as they don't cause the silk to snag. You can use masking tape if the piece of silk is not too big.

BRUSHES AND APPLICATORS Use a soft brush to apply the silk paints. Gutta is applied from a plastic applicator, which can be used alone or with a special nib. To avoid air bubbles in the gutta, turn the applicator up vertically at regular intervals. Always clean the applicator and nozzle with turpentine immediately after use to prevent them becoming blocked.

PAINTING THE LINGERIE

DESIGN A SIMPLE motif and draw it on a piece of paper. Use thick lines for the outline so that you can see them through the silk.

WASH THE SILK fabric or garment to remove any sizing or grease, using a gentle detergent in lukewarm water.

Roll the fabric in a towel and iron while it is still damp. Pin the silk on the frame, stretching it as you pin. Work from the center of one side out to the edge and then from the center to the other edge. Slip the design under the silk and tape it to the edges of the frame.

TRACE OVER THE design with the gutta, making sure there are no gaps. (If gaps are left, the silk paint will bleed through.) Make sure the gutta penetrates the silk through to the back. Check that the gutta is thick enough by holding the silk up to the light. If necessary, add more gutta. Leave the gutta to dry for about an hour, or speed up the process by using a hair dryer.

DIP A GOOD-QUALITY brush into the silk paints and apply the color. This is done not so much by painting, but by allowing the paint to diffuse from the brush onto the silk and up to the edge of the gutta. Rinse the brush between colors to eliminate any possible muddiness.

WHEN THE SILK painting is finished and dry, remove it from the frame and fix according to the paint manufacturer's instructions.

Silk boxer shorts can easily be decorated with silk paints, and the motif can be as restrained or as wild as you like

Labors of Love

During the eighteenth and nineteenth centuries, hearts were used as trade symbols in both America and Britain. Sailors who had long voyages would make elaborate Valentine pincushions to give to their sweethearts on their return to land. They would also fashion boxes into heart shapes and decorate them with shells.

Labors of love can take many forms. Most of these chosen here cost very little to make, but the investment of time makes them very precious, especially today, with our rushed lifestyles and reliance on store bought gifts. The pleasure of making these labors of love is equal to the pleasure of receiving them.

FRAMED
HEARTS

Appliqué is known to have existed as a craft from very early times, however, owing to the fragile nature of textiles, which are easily destroyed by sunlight and general wear and tear, most early examples of appliqué no longer exist. The earliest piece of appliqué work in existence is a ceremonial canopy dating from about 980 B.C. It is made from dyed gazelle hide, which has been decorated with many symbols from ancient Egypt.

Appliqué is a craft which spans history and continents. There are many different techniques and traditions, which in the past were often carried along trade routes. Often a technique from one part of the world might be altered slightly as the indigenous materials were different from one place to the next. Many nomadic tribes produced felt appliqué. In Siberia, Lapland, and Scandinavia, the fur and skin of caribou, reindeer, and seals were used to appliqué onto garments to add both decoration and extra thickness for warmth.

An "appliqué" is a picture made from applied fabrics and different

A variety of wonderful framed hearts made from solid fabric and embellished with appliquéd beads, buttons, and sequins

FABRIC
HEARTS

These beautiful fabric hearts are made using a combination of traditional appliqué techniques to produce a thoroughly modern piece of work. The two major techniques involved are three-dimensional appliqué and shadow work. Three-dimensional appliqué, or "stumpwork," was popular in Elizabethan England. Ornaments were raised in relief on a foundation of wool or cotton fiber, in the same way as this solid satin heart is set in a sea of translucent fabrics. Often the easiest way to achieve this effect is first to sew the empty shape onto a background, then slit through the background, insert the filling, and finally stitch up the hole.

Shadow work, as its name might suggest, is the application of opaque fabrics onto a background; these are then covered with layers of transparent and semi-transparent fabrics. This gives a very delicate impression, owing to the kind of fabrics used: organdy, voile, organza, net, and sheer synthetics. Remember that in shadow work the negative shapes can play as important a part in the design as the positive ones.

Left A display of romantic collage
heart cards

ROMANTIC PAPERCUTS

Papercutting is a craft that has its roots in a rural or folk way of life. It was found in village communities in the East in China, Japan and Vietnam, and in the West in Russia, Turkey, Mexico, Poland and other European countries, particularly in Switzerland. Although very different in style, the content of the papercuts is similar. The people in rural communities drew their inspiration from the same sources: their everyday lives and surroundings, plowing, animals, dancing, and flowers. Some papercuts depict people's occupations, such as thatching, spinning, farming, and woodcutting.

Papercuts were often made in the same way that we might make simple Christmas decorations, only to be put up for a few days and then discarded. Sometimes the papercuts were left unadorned; sometimes they were tinted and painted. A piece of calligraphy might be added in the form of a poem or inscription.

The Victorians practiced a slightly different form of papercutting, that of the silhouette portrait. This was particularly fashionable in seventeenth- and eighteenth-century Europe before photography was invented. They also made pinpricked papercuts by cutting, folding, and then pricking

Left Black and white heart-inspired papercuts mounted on contrasting card

out the designs using dressmaker's pins. This kind of papercut looks especially effective with light shining through it, for example, on a windowpane or as part of a lampshade.

MAKING A PAPERCUT

The papercuts featured here were inspired by the work of two renowned papercutters, Louis Saugy and Johann Jakob Hauswirth.

MATERIALS
EMBROIDERY SCISSORS
EXACTO KNIFE
SHARPENED PENCIL
TRACING PAPER
SKETCH PAD
CUTTING BOARD
MASKING TAPE

YOU MAY WISH to draw out your design in rough before you start and then transfer it, using tracing paper, or you may wish to work freehand. Start with simple designs and then move on to something slightly more complex. The tree of life is a symmetrical symbol common to all folk cultures. As with a stencil, make sure that you have plenty of "bridges" between each motif to hold the work together. Do not work on paper that is too thick or flimsy. If it is too thick, it will be difficult to cut; if it is too fine, it may rip while you are working.

FOLD THE PAPER in half and cut through two layers so that the papercut is symmetrical. Cut around the outer edge of the shape first, cutting away any excess paper. Then start cutting the detail. To cut the shapes in the center accurately you will need to use an exacto knife.

FOR AN INTRICATE, nonsymmetrical papercut, open it out at this stage and work on it in a single layer; otherwise, as with the symmetrical papercuts shown here, leave it folded. With either method, tape it to the cutting board with masking tape. Cut away the center pieces. Work systematically from the center outward, discarding bits of paper as you go. When you have cut away all the pieces, untape the papercut and frame it.

PIN-CUSHION HEARTS

Before 1820, when an Englishman invented a machine for making pins in one piece, they came in two pieces and the head had to be clamped onto the shaft. Being handmade, they were very expensive and highly prized. There were even proverbs written about pins:

"If you see a pin and let it lie,
You'll need a pin before you die."

The safekeeping of these precious objects, which could get lost so easily, inspired several inventions: pin boxes made from wood or silver, and pincushions. Paper, fabric, and needlepoint were all used to make pincushions, which came in a variety of shapes and sizes – hearts, stars, balls, and square pillow shapes being the most popular. The Victorians made heart-shaped pincushions out of a patchwork of brightly colored scraps. These were decorated with improving texts or tear-jerking mottos.

Pincushions have an enchanting history, from expressing the devotion of sailors on long voyages to their sweethearts to welcoming the arrival of a new baby

During the eighteenth and nineteenth centuries, the layette pillow became a fashionable gift for new mothers. These pillows were stuck with pins arranged to form a design or verse. A popular motto was "Welcome Little Stranger." Sometimes whole verses and very elaborate designs were used. The following lines come from Godey's *Lady's Book*, published in Philadelphia:

"May thy fragrance ever be
Like the rose bud in the tree,
With a lustre more sublime,
And thy every virtue shine."

These pincushions were often an extravagant combination of silk or satin in cream and ivory, decorated with lace, pretty ribbons, pins, and beads.

Sailors used to make padded hearts to give to their loved ones when they reached dry land. They would pad and appliqué shape upon shape until they had built up a kaleidoscope of patterns. They would then begin adding the ornamentation, often pinning beads through sequins. Surviving examples are very detailed, reflecting the long hours spent at sea.

Right These red velvet hearts make elegant pincushions but when threaded with red ribbon, are also wonderful as really unusual and sumptuous Christmas decorations

Far right A selection of antique beaded pincushions, which are now collector's items

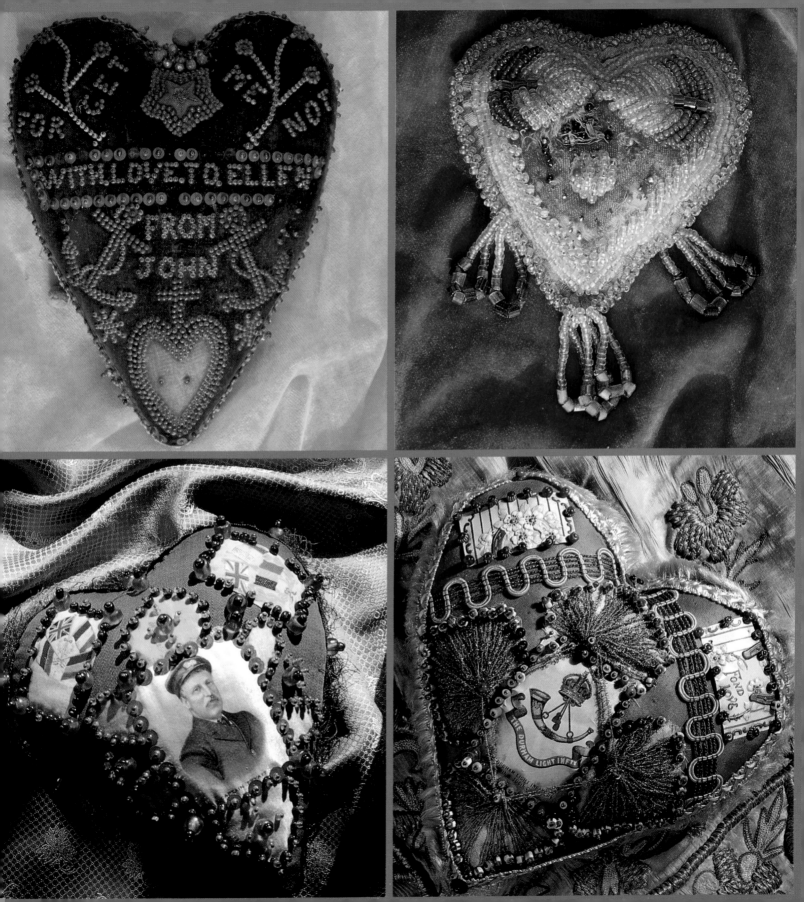

A KEEPSAKE PINCUSHION

Make your own keepsake pincushion either to give to your sweetheart or as a commemorative gift, using rich fabric such as velvet or brocade. For a special christening or wedding present, silk in ivory or cream might be more appropriate.

Use rustproof pins for the design on the pincushion. These are more expensive than ordinary pins, but they have larger heads and look more like handmade pins. Lace pins are extra-fine for use on delicate fabrics and can be added to complement the lace trimming. The best materials for filling the pincushion are sawdust or bran, which can be easily bought from a pet store.

MATERIALS
GRAPH PAPER
PAPER AND PENCIL
PAPER SCISSORS
DRESSMAKING SHEARS
20 IN./50 CM LINING
FABRIC
20 IN./50 CM RICH FABRIC
(SILK, VELVET)
SAWDUST OR BRAN FILLING
TISSUE PAPER
LARGE-HEADED SHORT
RUSTPROOF PINS
SEQUINS AND BEADS
(OPTIONAL)
LACE FOR EDGING
CORD AND TASSELS
(OPTIONAL)

The basic heart shape and the planned design on paper

The pincushion is filled with sawdust or bran to hold the pins firmly

Finish the pincushion with lace edging and decorative pins

Right The completed pincushion with its silver flowers made of individual pinheads – a delightful gift and useful sewing aid

USE GRAPH PAPER to work out your design, as you would for a needlepoint design. Each square is equivalent to a pin.

DRAW A HEART shape on paper (see page 125 for templates), cut it out, and use it as a pattern. Cut two hearts from lining fabric and two slightly smaller ones from the top fabric.

MAKE THE PINCUSHION pad by sewing together the two pieces of lining fabric, right sides facing, leaving a gap on one side for turning right side out. Turn through the gap, stuff with sawdust or bran, and sew up. You may need to use a knitting needle to push the filling into the point of the heart. Make the cover in the same way as the lining, leaving part of one side unstitched. Put the pincushion pad inside the cover. It should fit very tightly to produce a firm pincushion. Sew up the pincushion using hemstitch.

PLACE THE TISSUE paper over the design on the graph paper and trace it. Put the tissue paper on the pincushion and pin on the design through the paper. Remove the paper. This will be a slow and fiddly job. You can also add sequins and beads at this stage if you wish.

SEW THE LACE by hand around the edge of the pincushion, taking care to choose a lace that accords with the main fabric. Cream lace looks particularly fetching and gives the pincushion an antique look. Dot the lace with pins. You could add cord or tassels to the point of the heart as a decorative finish or leave it plain.

RED
ROSE
WREATH

Wreaths are as versatile as painting. They may be hung anywhere – on the back or front of a door as a friendly welcome, over a mantelpiece, or on the wall. The heart-shaped rose wreath featured here, for instance, would look as pretty on a hutch as in a bedroom.

When choosing flowers, remember that they are at their cheapest when they are in season. So although you can use flowers that have been artificially forced, they will be less robust and will not last as long as seasonal flowers. As you need quite a large number of flowers, it is obviously cheapest to use what is available from your own garden, if you have one. Otherwise, you could buy directly from flower wholesalers or special flower markets.

A rose wreath is particularly effective as the rose heads dry very well – so that you can keep the wreath for several months. Try making a wreath out of just miniature roses too, for a more delicate effect.

Left A traditional and romantic red rose wreath for Valentine's Day or a special birthday

Sealed
WITH A
Kiss

St. Valentine's Day is the traditional time for the exchange of mementoes between lovers. Today, it is easy to feel that the romance of its origins in ancient festivals and folklore is now becoming lost to commercialism. Whether you are sending a Valentine token to a lover or expressing special affection toward members of your family or to friends, bring back a special intimacy with your own handmade, heart-inspired gifts, cards, and packaging. Old boxes, brown paper, and scraps of fabric can be easily and stunningly transformed.

PASSIONATE GIFT WRAPS

The presentation of a gift is as important as the gift itself. One usually associates hearts with Valentine's Day, and they are traditionally depicted in vibrant reds. Yet why not introduce a change and keep to the heart theme, but use a subtle color scheme of old gold with purple, or black with gold? Use handmade papers or brown paper embossed with tiny gold stickers. Collect old boxes from candy, shoes, etc., and use these for gift wrapping. Stencil, print, or paint directly on the box or make wrapping paper to cover it.

Stencils can be made from paper doilies. Cut a heart from the center of the doily. Remove the center carefully and spray through the doily onto tissue paper to give a central slightly diffused-looking solid heart in gold, with a tracery design on the outside. If you wish to have more than one motif on your paper, cut heart shapes from several doilies and tape them together. Lay them on top of the tissue paper and spray through. The result will be a sheet of gold lacy-looking wrapping paper.

Alternatively, retrieve the piece you had previously discarded from the center of the paper doily and spray through it. You will then have a lacy heart surrounded by an area of solid gold. Repeat this pattern to cover the whole sheet of paper.

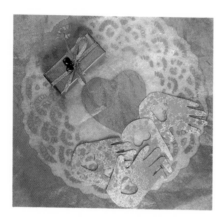

You can also make stencils by cutting heart shapes from paper or thin cardboard. Use spray paint to color the paper or sponge or apply with a stencil brush. Anchor the paper in position with masking tape. Remove the stencil carefully, making sure it doesn't smudge the paint as it is lifted.

Try a simple cardboard stencil with a wax crayon or felt-tipped pen on plain paper. Simply scribble within the heart shape back and forth to pattern the paper.

You do not need to buy expensive ribbons to tie your presents. You

Right and overleaf Some of the many ingenious ways in which you can adapt plain packaging, ribbon or tissue paper with heart stencils or gold hearts for a sumptuous and unique effect

can decorate plain ribbons or bias binding by drawing or stenciling small hearts. Use fabric pens or gold felt-tipped pens or glitter paints. The ends of the ribbon may even be decorated with tiny gold heart-shaped stickers.

If the image you require is less busy, wrap the present in plain tissue paper and then stick on a simple heart shape. This may be the doily heart you previously sprayed through, now gold, or a tissue paper heart in a contrasting color. Build up layers of tissue paper hearts to make a rosette.

If the present is an awkward shape, wrap it in a fabric bag. Decorate the fabric with fabric paint. Either sponge, stencil or potato-print the hearts onto the fabric. Once you have made up the bag, tie it closed with a length of string or ribbon or a decorated piece of bias binding.

Make heart-shaped gift tags from colored cardboard, and use lengths of ribbon or gold cord to attach them to the presents.

Collect heart-shaped beads, buttons, or even tree decorations and adapt them to the color you need by spraying or painting. If you can't find a heart-shaped motif to hang from the present, make your own from fine copper wire. You can then use it by itself or thread it with beads or sequins or cover it in foil.

DÉCOUPAGE DELIGHTS

The word "découpage" comes from the French verb *découper* - to cut out. It is the art of decorating a surface using paper cutouts. That is to say, illustrations and prints are chosen, cut out, and arranged to create a new design. Each piece is then glued in position and varnished or lacquered.

Well-executed découpage is often mistaken for painting. In fact, eighteenth-century découpeurs worked their craft with the very intention of imitating more expensive wares. At this time Japanese and Chinese lacquerware with its hand-painted motifs was very fashionable. Imitations of the lacquer furniture were often made from papier-mâché and decorated with découpage. This new art form, known as Art Provo or poor man's lacquer, was soon more popular than the furniture that it was trying to imitate.

Découpage is thought to have started in the late seventeenth century in Italy. It spread throughout Europe in the eighteenth century. It was known in the French court of Louis XVI, when young men would visit the ladies of the court, bringing gifts of original drawings and prints for them

Hearts have been used as the main motif on these magnificent découpage bowls

to cut up while they sat in their salons. It became a very popular hobby in Victorian England, so much so that the Victorians used to buy commercially packaged scraps which they combined to build up rich compositions on boxes and furniture.

WORKING THE DÉCOUPAGE

Use good-quality pictures to make your découpage. Save old wrapping paper, Christmas and birthday cards, and postcards. When designing, try to stick to a theme, for example, cherubs, flowers, or butterflies. As the varnish takes a long time to dry, it is worth working on two or three items at the same time.

The object to be covered in découpage must be well prepared. Make sure it is clean, and remove any labels. If it is made from wood, sand it smooth and fill any holes. Gather all your materials together and cut out each motif using small sharp scissors .

Arrange the motifs on the object until you have a pleasing design. Pick up one motif at a time, spread glue on the back of it, and press it firmly into position. As each piece is stuck on, press hard to get rid of any air bubbles and to create a smooth surface.

CUPID'S BOXES

These colorful hatboxes are all decorated with découpage, and they are stunning ornaments for your home or a lavish way of presenting a gift.

MATERIALS
BOX OR TIN TO DECORATE
PICTURES FOR DECORATION
SMALL SHARP SCISSORS
WALLPAPER PASTE, GLUE, OR
GLUE STICK
CLEAR VARNISH
FINE SANDPAPER
PAINTBRUSH AND TURPENTINE

PREPARE YOUR BOX or tin and glue on the trimmed pictures as described on page 115.

ONCE THE GLUE has dried, apply the varnish with a paintbrush. Do not varnish too thickly to avoid drips and runs. Leave each coat to dry before adding the next one. Apply alternate coats horizontally and vertically.

AFTER ABOUT 10 coats, sand lightly with wet sandpaper to remove dust and bubbles. Apply another 15 coats, sanding after every three or four and making sure the box is dry before varnishing again. Sand the last coat with a very fine sandpaper until it is dull. Finish with furniture polish or beeswax. Clean the paintbrush with turpentine to remove the varnish.

These hatboxes have been sanded and varnished to suggest an aged, painted surface

VALENTINE CARDS

During the Roman Lupercalian fertility rites held in honor of Juno, boys drew names of unmarried girls from a love urn. So popular was this early pagan ceremony that the Christian Church transferred elements of it to the feast day of St. Valentine, who was martyred at the same time of the year. Folklore, too, contains the idea of would-be lovers declaring themselves, as St. Valentine's Day is traditionally the day on which birds are said to choose their mates.

The idea of sending Valentine cards dates back to the sixteenth century, but it became the height of fashion in Victorian times, appealing to the Victorians' love of sentimentality. Verse writers were specially employed to turn the feelings and expressions of lovers and admirers into ornate and elevated verses. Copies of elaborate and prettily designed Victorian cards with their lace, flowers, and portraits are available today as an interesting alternative to modern mass-produced designs. Our beautiful fabric cards recapture the atmosphere of these original cards and, being hand-crafted, make an even more personal statement.

Left A selection of Victorian Valentine cards and modern-day cards, inspired by the delicacy and romance of these first Valentine messages

Layers of rich fabrics worked with machine embroidery create this original card

IRIDESCENT FABRIC CARDS

This card is made by layering pieces of fabric together and cutting away sections to reveal the colors beneath. Machine embroidery is used as it produces high-quality stitching speedily, and the heavy, multicolored silks create rich moody tones. The texture of the fabric is significant; 'shot' or 'cross-woven' silks add a depth of color far richer than that of a one-color-weave cloth.

Design ideas may often be triggered by the way colors and patterns combine together. New and interesting surfaces can be achieved all the time just by sewing shape over shape. One design motif blends into another so that a fleur-de-lys becomes a heart, which in turn may twist itself into a club. Grids and lattice-work structures with vines and creepers, twisting and weaving together over the surface, create patterns. Sunflowers, roses, stars, and planets also feature.

MATERIALS
RICH SHOT SILK – THREE DIFFERENT
COLORS, EACH APPROXIMATELY 7IN²/20 CM²
DRESSMAKING SHEARS
EMBROIDERY THREAD
EMBROIDERY SCISSORS
CARDBOARD MOUNT

CUT THE THREE different colored fabrics to the same size and shape. Place one on top of another and sew them together around the edge.

USING THE SEWING machine as you would a pencil, draw the design in a running stitch.

USING SMALL SHARP scissors such as nail or embroidery scissors, cut away through the design to reveal the fabric below or even the fabric below that. The result is that different elements of the design will appear as different colors.

FINISH THE CUT edges with a zigzag stitch or just leave them. Mount the fabric in a cardboard frame.

MOVING CUPID

This moving cupid will delight any child or make a really unusual Valentine card. It can be made very cheaply with just plywood and paint, or you can make it out of cardboard.

MATERIALS
THIN PLYWOOD (0.8MM BIRCH)
THICK WIRE 0.047 IN. (18 SWG)
THINNER WIRE 0.025 IN. (25 SWG)
1 IN./2.5 CM BRASS HINGE
MODEL PAINT – PINK,
WHITE, AND GOLD
GOLD METALLIC FELT-TIPPED PEN
SMALL, FLAT-NOSED PLIERS

PAPER SCISSORS OR EXACTO KNIFE
CLOTHESPIN OR BULLDOG CLIP
WOOD GLUE
PENCIL AND GRAPH PAPER
DENTAL FLOSS
THIN WHITE PAPER
2 SMALL WEDGES OF WOOD
(SUCH AS A MATCHSTICK)

TRACE AROUND THE main cupid body (x2), the leg (x1) and arm (x1), and heart (x2) on tracing paper. (See page 123 for designs). Then transfer them to plywood and cut out these shapes.

FIRST TAKE THE two heart shapes and make two holes in one of them as indicated on the pattern. Bend the thinner piece of wire back on itself with small flat-nosed pliers as indicated in diagram a and then push the wire through the holes in the heart. Bend another loop as in diagram b, which will eventually fit around the hinge.
TAKE THE THICKER wire and cut a piece 11 in./28 cm in length. Halfway along the wire, bend it around a piece of dowel or around a pair of round-nosed pliers to make a loop like a safety pin (see diagram c). Also bend one

Thick and thin wire is threaded through the heart-shaped bases of the cupid to form the frame for the body

The heart-shaped bases are glued together and secured with a clothespin while they are drying

Both sides of the cupid body are threaded through with wire and glued together. The second leg is added later

half of this wire back on itself to stick on the base. Then glue the flat piece of wire on the second heart with adhesive and glue the hearts together. Secure them with a clothespin or a bulldog clip until dry. Set aside.

NOW TAKE YOUR brass hinge and remove the center pin from it (this is best done by knocking it with a spare piece of wire or a thin nail). Put the hinge over the protruding thick wire as shown and then make an L-shaped bend in the end of it.

THREAD THE THIN wire ends through each front hinge hole and cut the wire ends off at the end of the hinge, so they lie next to (but not through) the back holes. Tie the two parts of the thin wire together on each side by threading dental floss through each back hole with a double knot. This allows free movement of the hinge (see diagram c).

NOW TAKE THE two cupid bodies, and the separate arm and leg. Make a hole with a compass point as indicated on the shoulder of the cupid. Thread the cupid through the thin wire frame and push the thicker wire through the hole you have just made (see diagram c). Coat the second cupid with glue and thread through the wire on the other side to make a sandwich and press them together. Hold with a clothespin until dry.

GLUE THE SMALL wooden wedge onto the leg to form a gusset. Now glue the cutout leg to this gusset as shown in diagram d. Then make two holes with

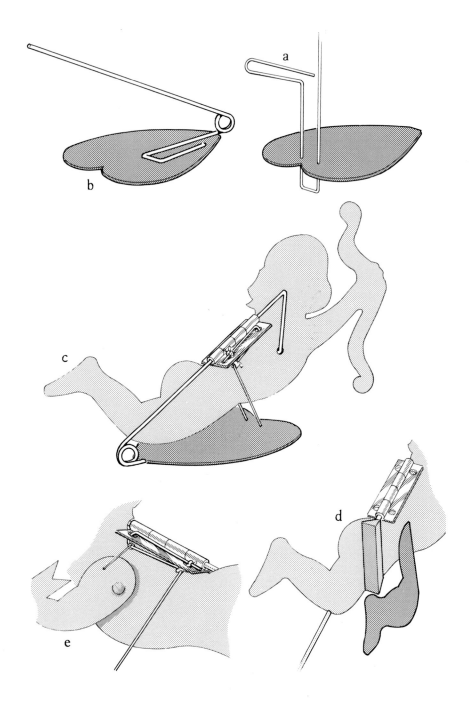

a compass in the top of the cutout arm as shown, in each end of the bow and one hole in the arrow. Tie a knot in the dental floss and thread it through the hole in the arm, so that the knot is on the inner side of the arm (diagram e). Then take it through the front hole of the hinge and tie it, so that when the hinge goes up, it pulls the arm up, too. Then push the thick wire through the other hole in the arm.

SLIP ON A bead or a blob of glue to cover the exposed sharp end of the wire. Then thread dental floss through the arrow and bow as shown and tie at each end. As a final touch, put a small wedge of wood on the base of the heart to allow the arm to swing down lower (see photograph right).

FOR THE WINGS, cut out four large wings and two small ones from typing paper. The large wings are then doubled up for strength. Glue one of the wings above and one below the hinge, taking care not to impede the mechanism. Then cover the wire with the smaller wing, but again do not glue the paper directly to the mechanism – glue it instead to the wing below and cover the hinge.

FINALLY, PAINT THE whole cupid white and leave it for six hours to dry. Add the pink and gold decoration as shown. Decorate the wings with a gold felt-tip pen.

Right The completed painted cupid and the trace-off cupid pattern. Remember to trace two of everything except the separate arm and leg

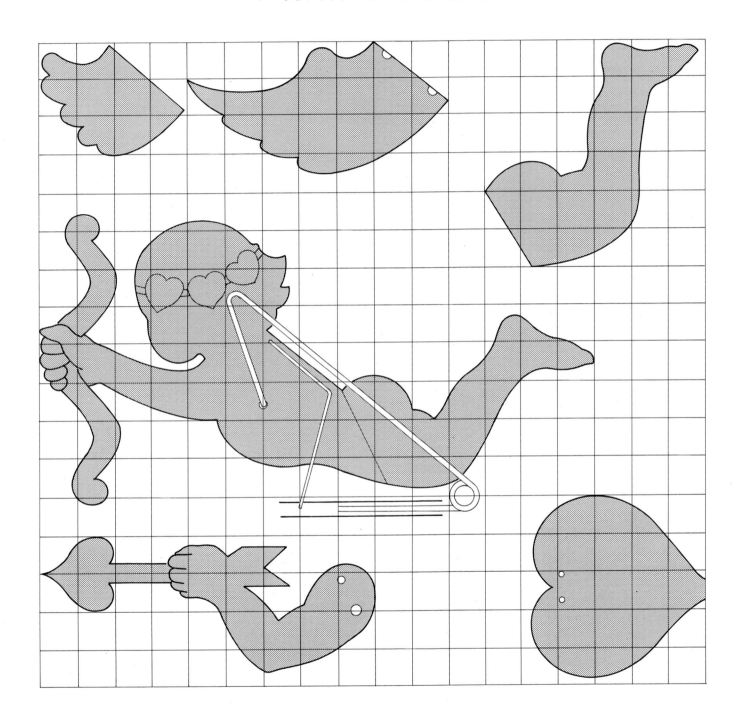

PRACTICALITIES

DRAWING HEARTS

A heart is one of the most difficult shapes to draw freehand if you wish it to be symmetrical. There are many different heart shapes in this book. Some are wide, such as those in the wreaths, while others are elongated, as in the rugs of Annie Sherburne. A variety of templates are printed here which you can trace or photocopy and cut out. A simple way of obtaining a symmetrical heart is to fold a piece of paper in half and draw half a heart with the point and the indent on the fold and cut out through both thicknesses of paper. Open up to produce the complete heart.

SEWING HEARTS

When sewing a heart shape, for example an appliquéd or patchwork heart, it is best to clip all around the seam allowance as this will help the fabric to give when the seams are turned under or sewn together.

Another trick is to taper the seam allowance toward the indentation at the top of the heart and at the point so there is not too much bulk of fabric. A dab of glue will stop fraying and hold the tiny seam allowance firmly in place.

When making a heart-shaped pillow or pillow cover, leave the opening for turning right side out on one of the side seams. Sew a double line of stitches to strengthen the seams and then clip into the indentation and point, to relieve any pulling. Cut away any excess seam allowance.

STENCILING HEARTS

The wonderful toy box on pages 32-35 has been covered in heart and arrow stencils. The patterns for these are reproduced on page 126 so that you can trace them yourself. When making a stencil, you need to buy some stencil paper or acetate which is water resistant. Trace your design on your stencil paper, and then cut the shapes out with a very sharp exacto knife. It always helps to cut toward you as you go, making sure you cut in a continuous line, never lift the knife until the cut area is completed.

When you have your master heart and arrow stencil, you need to test the colors first before applying them to a chosen surface. Always remember to use just a little paint and choose a fast-drying acrylic or stencil paint. Affix the stencil with masking tape to your surface and apply the paint with a stiff paint brush. Keep a cloth next to you so that you can dab the bristles of the brush into it each time you add paint. The brush head should look almost dry.

When you remove the stencil, be sure to lift it vertically so as not to smudge the design. Wipe off any excess paint so that the stencil is ready to use again. Use a fresh brush for each color and make sure the tip is dry – a wet brush will smear the paint. For the toy box, metallic felt-tipped pens were used to outline the lid and the edges, and these are also ideal for filling in stencils for a really dramatic effect.

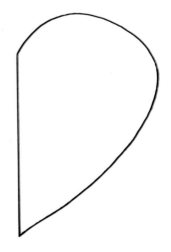

Heart template for sweetheart quilt,
page 26

Heart and arrow stencil template for toy box, page 34

ACKNOWLEDGMENTS

The publisher would like to thank the following people for their contributions:
Candace Bahouth (Cupid Cushion, pp14-17), Ebenezer Chapel, Pilton, Somerset BA4 4BR, (0749 890 433)

Henrietta Bathurst (Quilt, pp24-27; Beaded Denims and Sneakers, pp32, 33, 40, 41), (071 352 4177)

Fiona Barnett (Lavender and Rose Wreaths, pp100-105), Manic Botanic Ltd, 2 Silver Place, London W1R (071 287 9856)

Sarah Beresford (Tie and Hanky, p79), 50b Holmewood Road, Brixton Hill, London SW2 3RR, (081 674 2411)

Janet Bolton (Framed Pictures, pp84-87), 40 Aislibie Road, Lee Green, London SE12 8QQ, (081 318 3743)

Jan Bridge (Pincushion, pp96-97; Christening Set, pp40-43)

Mike Candler (Découpage Bowls, pp114-115), (0533 743342)

Caroline Goodwin (Pincushions p95), Blackheath Village, London SE3

Lesley Harle (Loving Plates, pp62-65), Flat 3, 11 Croft Road, Godalming, Surrey GU7 1BF, (0483 420179)

Karen Holt (Brooches, pp76-78), 232 Turton Road, Bradshaw, Bolton BL2 3EE, (0204 591878)

Sarah King (Organza Mats, pp58-61), Waterside, 99 Rotherhithe Street, London SE16 4NF, (071 237 0017)

Meryl Lloyd (Gift Wraps, pp110-13)

Edy Lyngaas (Sweater, pp68-73), 83 Northchurch Road, London N1 3NU, (071 226 6586)

Abigail Mill (Collage Hearts, pp88-89), Glebe Cottage, Church Road, Spexhall, Halesworth, Suffolk IP19 0RQ, (0986 873316)

Diana Miller (Herb Wreath, pp100-1), Primrose Cottage, Church Lane, Chey-next-the-sea, Holt, Norfolk NR25 7TZ

Lorna Moffat (Iridescent Fabric Card, pp118-19), 38 Canon Woods Way, Kennington, Ashford, Kent TN24 9QY, (0233 638508)

Painted Ladies (Papier-Mâché Mirror and Vase, pp10-13), 6c Warwick Road, Ealing, London W5 3XJ, (081 840 0416)

Juliette Pearce (Papier-Mâché Jewels, pp74-75), Cross Street Studios, 14 Cross Street, Hove BN3 1AJ, (0273 725321)

Trisha Rafferty (Hat Pins, Pin Boxes, pp66-67; p82-83, 108-9), 54 Byron Street, Hove BN3 5BB

Sandra Rangecroft (Dried Flowers, pp106-7), Orchard House, Mortlake Road, Kew Gardens, Surrey TW9 4AS, (081 392 9929)

Deborah Schnebeeli-Morrell (Papercut Cards, pp90-91), 10 York Rise, London NW5 1SS

Annie Sherburne (Heart Rugs, pp18-19), Waterside, 99 Rotherhithe Street, London SE16 4NF, (071 237 5630)

Jenny Tapping (Heart Card, p118), Rumins Cottage, St Ruan, Ruan Minor, Helston, Cornwall TR12 7JS, (0326 290 84)

Tobias and the Angel (Doll's Quilt, pp20-23; Pincushions, pp92-94), 68 White Hart Lane, Barnes, London SW13 0PZ, (081 878 8902)

Stewart Walton (Toy Box, pp32-35), Mike Heighington Designs, 948-950 High Road, Finchley, London N12 9RX

Emma Whitfield (Hatboxes, pp116-117), 3 Tresidder House, Clapham Park Estate, Poynders Road, London SW4

Arthur Wilson (Moving Cupid, pp120-23), 22 Wingate Road, London W9 0UR, (081 743 0522)

The publishers would like to thank the following for their help with props:

The American Country Collection Ltd, 28 Baker Street, Weybridge, Surrey KT13 8AU

Art Graphic, Unit 2, Poulton Close, Dover, Kent CT17 0HL, (Pebeo silk paints)

Global Village, 247-249 Fulham Road, London SW3 (071 376 5363)

Idencroft Herbs, Staplehurst, Kent (0580 891432)

Italian Papershop, 1 Brompton Arcade, London SW3, (071 589 1668)

Offray Ribbons, Fir Tree Place, Church Road, Ashford, Middlesex TW15 2PH

The Shaker Shop, 25 Harcourt Street, London W1H 1DT, (071 724 7672)

Stitches and Daughters, 5-7 Tranquil Vale, London SE3 (081 852 8507)

Tie Rack, (Silk boxer shorts)

Tobias and the Angel, 68 White Hart Lane, Barnes, London SW13 0PZ, (081 878 8902)

Wenna Bishop Glass, 18 Southwell Road, Camberwell, London SE5 9PG, (071 737 4066)

The author would also like to thank:
Denise Bates and Louise Simpson for being such kind, encouraging editors. Debbie for her lush and lovely photographs. Mary for making the book a visual treat. Vanessa and her new baby, and Kit and Olivia for designing the book. Esther Burt, Katie Scampton, Jan Bridge and Lena Ilyschin for all their help making things. Jane Suthering for writing the recipes and cooking the delicious food. Maureen Brampton at The Bluecoat Display Centre, Bluecoat Chambers, School Lane, Liverpool, and everyone at the Victoria and Albert Museum Shop and the Crafts Council for all their help in finding contributors.

INDEX